Breaking Barriers in Corporate America:
Winning in a
White Man's World
By Catrese Kilgore

Contents

Prelude: Failed Dreams to Breaking Barriers

In the dimly lit room, the pages of a life's story turn. A story marked by the ink of ambition and the fire of resilience. It's a narrative etched in the pursuit of excellence, a journey through corporate corridors, where the echoes of breaking barriers and building wealth resound. Welcome to my world, a world where dreams defy the odds and destinies are meticulously crafted.

A world where the deck is stacked against you, where the hurdles seem insurmountable, and the odds are whispered as unachievable. This is the world I entered—an environment where success was often reserved for the few, where preconceived notions and stereotypes clouded the path to greatness.

But I've never been one to bow to expectations. My journey is a testament to the power of determination and the relentless pursuit of excellence. In the pages of "Breaking Barriers in Corporate America: Winning in a White Man's World," I invite you to walk alongside me—a journey that transcends the boundaries of race and gender and speaks to the universal quest for success.

This is the story of how I navigated a world that tried to define me and how I defied those definitions. It's a prelude to another chapter in my life, "Breaking Barriers and Building Wealth," where I share the financial strategies that helped me achieve prosperity.

You'll accompany me from PwC to Ernst & Young to Sterling Group, witnessing the calculated risks I took, the strategic moves I made, and the power of leveraging job offers to secure what I deserved. It's a story of resilience, of embracing change, and of achieving excellence in the face of adversity.

But this isn't just my story; it's a guidebook for your own journey. Through practical advice, motivational quotes, and personal anecdotes, I offer you a roadmap to overcome obstacles and achieve your dreams in a world that may try to hold you back. Your past does not define your future, and with unwavering commitment, you too can break barriers and build wealth.

So, as we embark on this transformative journey together, remember that within you lies the potential to excel beyond your wildest dreams. My story is a testament to that potential—a reminder that breaking barriers and building wealth are not mere dreams but the destiny that awaits you.

Continued Success,

Catrese Kilgore

Chapter 1: A Rocky Start

In the dimly lit, weathered living room of our small, rented home, I sat alone, a young girl with big dreams, surrounded by uncertainty and despair. The walls bore the scars of time, their once-vibrant paint now faded and peeling. Threadbare curtains struggled to filter the harsh sunlight that seeped through the cracks. This was my childhood home, a place where dreams were born but often remained unfulfilled.

A Difficult Childhood

My name is Catrese, and the backdrop of my journey toward a successful accounting career was a challenging and modest upbringing. I grew up in a neighborhood where financial stability was an elusive concept. My family lived paycheck to paycheck, and my mother, a tireless teacher, raised four children as a single parent. Our home, a small, cramped space, mirrored the limitations of our financial circumstances.

The paint on the walls had faded to a muted beige, the once-sturdy furniture now showing signs of wear and tear. The wooden floors creaked with every step, a constant reminder of the aging structure that housed our dreams and aspirations. The kitchen, though small, was the heart of our home, where my mother worked tirelessly to put food on the table, often with limited resources.

Repeated Cycles of Poverty

At the age of 18, I embarked on a new chapter in life, determined to break free from the cycle of poverty that had plagued my family for generations. I enrolled in college with dreams of a brighter future. However, the path was not without its challenges. Balancing the demands of academics, work, and newfound independence was a daunting task. Nevertheless, I persevered, driven by the belief that education was the key to a better life.

But life took an unexpected turn at 21 when I made the difficult decision to drop out of college. It was a choice born out of necessity, as I was about to start a family with my husband. We faced the immense challenge of providing for our two children, and my dreams of higher education took a backseat to the immediate needs of our growing family.

The Struggles of Parenthood

As young parents, my husband and I faced the harsh reality of financial instability. We worked tirelessly to make ends meet, often taking on multiple jobs to provide for our children. The dreams of owning a home or pursuing a fulfilling career seemed distant, overshadowed by the daily grind of survival.

The Turning Point

Yet, despite the challenges, a determination to change our circumstances burned within me. I couldn't accept that my children would face the same cycle of poverty that had haunted my family for generations. At the age of 28, I made a life-changing decision — a decision that would set me on the path to realizing my dreams.

I resolved to return to college, to pick up the dreams I had put on hold, and to pursue a career in accounting. The goal was set: to graduate before my 30th birthday, a milestone that held both personal significance and the promise of a brighter future for my family.

Facing Doubters and Naysayers

As I embarked on this life-altering journey, I encountered skepticism and doubt from those around me. Friends and family, while well-intentioned, questioned the feasibility of my decision. They pointed to my past struggles and responsibilities as reasons to abandon my aspirations. It was a pivotal moment, a crossroads where I had to choose between succumbing to the negativity or forging ahead with unwavering resolve.

The Resilience to Never Give Up

In that dimly lit living room, surrounded by faded walls and the weight of past struggles, I embraced the words of Harriet Beecher Stowe: "Never give up, for that is just the place and time that the tide will turn." These words became my mantra, propelling me forward with an unyielding spirit. Each setback only fueled my determination to succeed. With sheer grit and relentless effort, I tackled my studies, juggled motherhood, and worked part-time jobs to make ends meet.

The Road Ahead

This chapter sets the stage for the remarkable journey that lies ahead—a journey marked by resilience, determination, and an unwavering commitment to turning dreams into reality. The road ahead is rocky, filled with obstacles that would test the very core of my being. However, it's a road I willingly traverse, knowing that each step brings me closer to a destiny I've dared to envision.

Join me as we explore the highs and lows of my quest to excel in the world of accounting, where dreams intersect with destiny, and where the pursuit of success often begins in the face of adversity.

Chapter 2: The Power of Resilience

My journey was a testament to resilience—a story fueled by an unwavering promise I had made to myself: never to give up, regardless of the obstacles before me. It was this determination that propelled me back to college at the age of 28, despite the chorus of naysayers that surrounded me. In the end, I not only graduated but did so as the top student in the business school. How did I achieve this? It was a combination of my father's sage advice, a meticulous approach to goal-setting, and the unwavering support of my husband and three small children.

A Father's Wisdom

My father had always been a wellspring of wisdom, and his words continued to guide me throughout my life. "Be the best in whatever you do," he would say. "Be the leader, not the follower. Have the knowledge, have the power." These pearls of wisdom were more than just words; they were a blueprint for success.

Writing Down My Goals

One of the most valuable lessons my father had imparted to me was the importance of setting clear goals. From an early age, he encouraged me to write down my aspirations, to commit them to paper, and in doing so, to make them tangible and real. And so, armed with determination, I began by writing down my ultimate goal: to graduate with a degree in accounting.

With that overarching goal in mind, I took a page from my father's book, quite literally. I began breaking down this monumental task into smaller, manageable steps. I wrote out sub-goals, class by class, semester by semester. Each course became a milestone on my journey, a step towards my larger goal.

As I worked my way through each semester, I meticulously crossed off the classes I had completed and marked the ones that lay ahead. This methodical approach not only provided me with a clear roadmap but also a sense of accomplishment with each step forward.

Overcoming Doubt

The doubters and naysayers that surrounded me persisted, but their voices grew faint as my determination grew stronger. My father's teachings and my written goals became my armor against negativity. Each time I faced doubt, I would revisit my written goals, a tangible reminder of what I was working toward.

A Supportive Husband

My journey was not one I undertook alone. At my side was my husband, a pillar of support and encouragement. He not only shared the responsibilities of raising our three small children but also provided unwavering emotional support. His belief in my abilities and his dedication to our shared dreams gave me the strength to continue, even on the toughest of days.

A Juggling Act

Balancing the demands of academia, motherhood, and part-time work was no small feat. It was a juggling act that often required late-night study sessions and early morning childcare duties. There were moments of exhaustion and doubt, but the desire to create a better future for my family pushed me forward.

I found solace and motivation in a quote by the renowned American poet, Maya Angelou: "You may encounter many defeats, but you must not be defeated. In fact, it may be necessary to encounter the defeats so you can know who you are, what you can rise from, how you can still come out of it."

These words resonated deeply within me. They became a mantra, a source of strength, reinforcing my belief that resilience in the face of adversity was the key to realizing my dreams.

Graduating at the Top

Against all odds, I reached that defining moment — graduation day. Not only did I complete my journey, but I also did so as the top student in the business school. It was a triumph of resilience, a testament to the power of setting clear goals, and the unwavering commitment to see them through.

The Resilience of Goal-Setting

This chapter serves as a testament to the resilience that resides within all of us. It demonstrates that when we combine determination with a systematic approach to goal-setting, we can conquer even the most formidable challenges. My father's guidance, along with my commitment to writing down and pursuing my goals, paved the way for my success and would continue to shape my journey in the field of accounting. It was a lesson that would carry me through the many challenges and triumphs that lay ahead, ultimately propelling me toward my dreams.

Chapter 3: The Pursuit of Excellence

Entering the corporate world at a prestigious firm like PricewaterhouseCoopers (PwC) marked a pivotal moment in my journey. As a Black woman, I quickly realized that the path to success required not only striving to be the best but also taking ownership of my career, stepping out of my comfort zone, fitting in, and building meaningful connections with peers. This chapter explores these facets of my corporate experience, enriched with motivational quotes that shed light on the unique challenges and triumphs of being Black in Corporate America.

A New Beginning

The moment I walked through the polished glass doors of PwC, I felt the weight of the opportunities and challenges that lay ahead. The towering skyscrapers, the bustling professional energy, and my impeccably dressed colleagues—all were part of a world that promised prestige and accomplishment. It was a world I was determined to navigate and excel in.

As a Black woman, I understood that I was entering a corporate realm where representation was often lacking. It was a double-edged sword—while the diversity of thought and perspective I brought to the table was invaluable, it also meant that I had to work twice as hard to prove my worth. The quote by the iconic Oprah Winfrey served as both inspiration and a stark reminder: "Excellence is the best deterrent to racism or sexism."

Owning My Career

From day one, I embraced the challenge of striving for excellence. I knew that by consistently outperforming expectations, I could break through the barriers that might have otherwise held me back. It was a commitment not just to myself but to those who would come after me.

One of the most valuable lessons I learned early on was the importance of taking ownership of my career. I realized that my success was in my hands. As Oprah Winfrey once said, "You are responsible for your life. You can't keep blaming somebody else for your dysfunction." I knew that it was up to me to chart my path and make the most of every opportunity.

Success rarely thrives within the confines of comfort. I had to push myself to embrace challenges and seize opportunities, even when they seemed daunting. Eleanor Roosevelt's words resonated with me: "You gain strength, courage, and confidence by every experience in which you really stop to look fear in the face. You must do the thing you think you cannot do."

The Art of Fitting In

In a corporate world where diversity was a precious asset, I recognized the importance of fitting in while staying true to myself. Finding the balance between cultural identity and corporate culture was an art I had to master. Toni Morrison's words became a guiding principle: "Definitions belong to the definers, not the defined." It was my role to define my place in the corporate landscape.

Building meaningful connections with my peers was a cornerstone of my journey. It wasn't just about networking; it was about forming bonds that would support and elevate me. The African proverb, "If you want to go fast, go alone. If you want to go far, go together," reminded me of the power of collaborative relationships.

The Role of Mentorship

Navigating this corporate terrain was not a solitary journey. I was fortunate to have mentors — individuals who recognized my potential and were willing to guide me. As the famous poet Langston Hughes once said, "Hold fast to dreams, for if dreams die, life is a broken-winged bird that cannot fly." My mentors were the wind beneath my wings, propelling me to greater heights.

The challenges I faced were not insurmountable, but they were real. I encountered moments of implicit bias, where my ideas were met with skepticism or my achievements were downplayed. But I refused to be discouraged. Instead, I harkened to the words of Maya Angelou: "You may not control all the events that happen to you, but you can decide not to be reduced by them."

Defying Expectations

My commitment to excellence began to yield results. I defied expectations and broke through barriers that had seemed unyielding. Each success, no matter how small, was a testament to the power of resilience and a reminder that excellence transcends stereotypes.

I couldn't ignore the subtle biases I encountered at times, where my ideas were met with skepticism or my achievements were downplayed. But I refused to be discouraged. As Maya Angelou wisely stated, "You may not control all the events that happen to you, but you can decide not to be reduced by them."

Being a Black woman in corporate America was not just about personal success; it was about paving the way for others who aspired to follow a similar path. As the pioneering astronaut Mae Jemison once said, "Never limit yourself because of others' limited imagination; never limit others because of your own limited imagination."

The Journey Continues

This chapter serves as a reminder that excellence is not only a choice but a potent tool for change. It illustrates the importance of owning one's career, embracing discomfort, fitting into a corporate landscape while preserving individuality, and building meaningful connections. My journey was far from over, and the challenges I encountered would only serve as stepping stones to even greater achievements. As I continued to pursue excellence, I knew that I was not only shaping my own destiny but also influencing the future of those who dared to dream beyond the constraints of convention.

Chapter 4: The Art of Building Relationships

In the dynamic world of corporate America, the art of building relationships is often the linchpin of success. This chapter delves deeply into the significance of networking, forming meaningful connections, and mastering the principles outlined in Dale Carnegie's timeless classic, "How to Win Friends and Influence People." It's a journey that highlights the transformative power of relationships, underscoring the pivotal role they played in my career, and the resilience it took to overcome an early setback.

A Humbling Start

The beginning of my career at PricewaterhouseCoopers (PwC) was marked by relentless dedication and unwavering commitment to excellence. I poured my heart and soul into my work, aiming to be the best accountant I could be. But despite my best efforts, my initiation into PwC began with a jarring revelation. I was ranked below average compared to my peers. It was a crushing blow, and I felt as though I had hit a wall. I found myself in an unexpected and disheartening position.

The Temptation to Quit

In the face of this setback, a sense of desolation began to creep in. I questioned my abilities, my choices, and my place within the corporate world. The temptation to quit and abandon my aspirations was tantalizingly close. The disappointment was almost overwhelming.

At my lowest ebb, I turned to the one person who had been my unwavering source of support—my husband. As we sat in our small, dimly lit living room, I poured out my frustration and despair. I confessed that I was ready to give up, convinced that I didn't have what it took to succeed in this competitive corporate arena.

My husband, a wellspring of strength and resilience in his own right, listened patiently. With a calm and steady voice, he reminded me of the challenges we had overcome together— of the times when we faced financial hardships, when we were struggling to make ends meet, and when we had to scrape by to provide for our children. He said, "Catrese, we've been through far worse than this, and we've come out stronger every time. This is just another challenge on our journey. Don't give up now."

Seeking Guidance from Mentors

With renewed determination and a sense of perspective, I decided to seek guidance from my mentors. I approached them with humility, admitting my struggles and the disappointment of my low ranking. Their response was a beacon of hope.

One of my mentors, who had been instrumental in my growth, reminded me of a treasure I had encountered earlier but hadn't fully appreciated — Dale Carnegie's "How to Win Friends and Influence People." This timeless masterpiece contained invaluable principles for building meaningful relationships, both in the professional world and in life.

Dale Carnegie's Wisdom

Two of the principles from Carnegie's book that left an indelible mark on my journey were:

- Show Genuine Interest: I learned the power of showing a sincere interest in others.
- Give Honest and Sincere Appreciation: Carnegie's wisdom underscored the

significance of expressing genuine appreciation.

Rather than focusing on self-promotion, I began actively listening, empathizing, and seeking to understand the perspectives and goals of my colleagues. By becoming genuinely interested in their lives, I forged deeper connections that transcended superficial interactions.

Carnegie's words illuminated my path: "You can make more friends in two months by becoming interested in other people than you can in two years by trying to get other people interested in you."

I made it a point to acknowledge the contributions of my colleagues openly and sincerely. Whether through a kind word, a note of thanks, or public recognition, I celebrated the efforts of those around me. This simple act of appreciation fostered a sense of camaraderie and strengthened our professional bonds.

The Personal PR Campaign

Embracing the wisdom of Dale Carnegie, I embarked on a personal PR campaign during my second year at PwC. I knew I needed to not only excel in my technical skills but also build genuine connections with my colleagues. I began by showing a sincere interest in their lives, goals, and aspirations. I asked my peers, my in-charges, my managers and even the partners for one-on-one meetings. Everyone is willing to walk to get Starbucks, especially if you are willing to treat. I prepared brief stories of what I would talk about and a long list of questions to keep whoever I was with talking about themselves. I actively listened, empathized, and sought ways to support them in their own journeys.

The transformation that followed was nothing short of remarkable. The once distant colleagues became allies and supporters. I was being picked up on the elite jobs in the office and was invited to all the happy hours. The camaraderie that grew out of these connections created a completely different work environment, where we all felt more comfortable. It was a testament to the truth in Zig Ziglar's words: "You don't have to be great to start, but you have to start to be great."

The Early Promotion

As my second year at PwC drew to a close, I received the news that I had been early promoted. The same human resource manager that told me I was ranked low the year before was now telling me about my miraculous turn-around. It was a momentous achievement, a tangible testament to the power of building genuine relationships and demonstrating a sincere interest in others. This promotion was going to be one step further to financial security for my family. And to think, I had almost quit, just one year before.

The Journey Continues

This chapter underscores the transformative power of relationships in the corporate landscape. It emphasizes the wisdom of Dale Carnegie and the importance of mastering the principles in "How to Win Friends and Influence People." My journey serves as a testament to the profound impact that genuine interest in others can have on one's career. As I continued to build and nurture relationships, I knew that the path to success was not just about individual achievement but also about the collaborative strength of the connections I forged along the way. In the words of Helen Keller, "Alone, we can do so little; together, we can do so much."

Chapter 5: Emotional Intelligence and Cultural Dexterity

As I journeyed through the corridors of corporate America, the significance of two attributes became increasingly apparent—emotional intelligence (EQ) and cultural dexterity. This chapter aims to provide a comprehensive understanding of the profound importance of these qualities, delving into how they have not only shaped my career but also enriched my life. Through personal anecdotes, valuable insights, and practical examples from the world of public accounting, I endeavor to illuminate the significance of navigating the complex terrain of emotions and cultures in the professional realm.

The Essence of Emotional Intelligence

Emotional intelligence, often referred to as EQ, became a cornerstone of my approach to corporate life. It wasn't just about understanding and managing emotions; it was about harnessing them to foster productive and empathetic interactions. EQ wasn't merely a skill; it was a way of life.

Consider a pivotal client meeting I encountered early in my career. Tensions were running high, deadlines were looming like dark clouds, and frustrations were palpable. Rather than reacting defensively to the mounting stress, I took a moment to acknowledge the emotions in the room. Practicing active listening and offering empathy to the client's concerns, I realized that this simple act of emotional intelligence de-escalated the tension and allowed us to work collaboratively to find a solution. It was a stark reminder of the power EQ wields in even the most challenging of professional circumstances.

Cultivating Cultural Dexterity

Cultural dexterity, the ability to adapt to different cultural contexts, was another skill that I honed over the years. As a Black woman in a predominantly white corporate world, I often found myself in situations where cultural differences became apparent. Rather than shying away from these differences, I embraced them as opportunities for growth.

One of the most impactful lessons I learned was the importance of being comfortable with discomfort. Cultural dexterity wasn't about pretending that differences didn't exist; it was about acknowledging them and finding ways to bridge the gaps. It meant having candid conversations about biases, stereotypes, and unconscious prejudices that might affect decision-making. It was about fostering an environment where everyone felt seen, heard, and valued.

Lessons Learned

- Lesson 1: Self-Awareness is the Foundation
    - One of the key lessons I learned from EQ was the importance of self-awareness. It was the cornerstone of emotional intelligence, empowering me to manage my reactions, remain calm under pressure, and build trust with colleagues and clients alike. By understanding the emotions driving the decisions of those around me, I could tailor my communication and approach to foster productive and positive interactions.

- Lesson 2: Empathy Fuels Connection
    - Empathy was the bridge that connected me to others on a profound level. It wasn't just about sympathizing with someone's feelings; it was about truly understanding their perspective and validating their experiences. Empathy transcended boundaries, making it possible to build deep, lasting connections with colleagues, clients, and team members from diverse backgrounds.
- Lesson 3: Inclusivity Drives Innovation
    - Cultural dexterity taught me that diversity wasn't just a buzzword—it was an engine of innovation. By actively seeking out and embracing diverse perspectives, teams could harness the power of collective creativity. It was in the intersections of different cultures and backgrounds that the most innovative solutions often emerged.
- Lesson 4: Discomfort is the Catalyst for Growth

o Perhaps one of the most enduring lessons was the value of discomfort. It was in moments of discomfort that I experienced the most significant personal and professional growth. Embracing uncomfortable conversations, challenging biases, and stepping outside my comfort zone led to profound transformations in both my career and my worldview.

A Catalyst for Change

Being a Black woman in corporate America also provided me with a unique opportunity to help my superiors and managers understand cultural differences and dexterity. Through open dialogue and education, I encouraged them to see the value of diversity and inclusion. I shared my experiences and those of my colleagues, shedding light on the challenges and triumphs that come with different cultural backgrounds.

One powerful quote that resonated with me during this journey was from Audre Lorde: "It is not our differences that divide us. It is our inability to recognize, accept, and celebrate those differences." I firmly believed that by embracing and celebrating our differences, we could create a workplace that thrived on diversity and benefited from a multitude of perspectives.

The Impact on My Career

Embracing emotional intelligence and cultural dexterity had a profound impact on my career. It allowed me to navigate the complex landscape of corporate America with grace and finesse. It also opened doors to opportunities I might not have otherwise encountered. I was entrusted with leadership roles that required not only technical expertise but also a deep understanding of the people and cultures I interacted with.

This chapter underscores the transformative power of emotional intelligence and cultural dexterity in the professional world. It emphasizes the wisdom gained from navigating emotions and embracing cultural differences. My journey serves as a testament to the enduring value of these qualities, and I continue to champion their importance as I progress through my career.

In the words of Maya Angelou, "We all should know that diversity makes for a rich tapestry, and we must understand that all the threads of the tapestry are equal in value no matter their color." As I continue to weave my unique thread into the corporate tapestry, I am committed to fostering a culture of empathy, understanding, and inclusivity—a culture where emotional intelligence and cultural dexterity are not just buzzwords but lived principles that shape a brighter future for us all.

Chapter 6: Taking Calculated Risks

In the intricate web of corporate America, my journey was a dance between ambition, financial challenges, and strategically calculated risks. This chapter delves deeper into the calculated risks I undertook, emphasizing the pivotal decisions and transformative moments that defined my path. It serves not only as a chronicle of experiences but also as a comprehensive guide for those navigating the competitive world of business. From a Black woman's perspective working at an accounting firm with aspirations of making partner, this chapter is enriched with personal anecdotes, motivational quotes, and insights that illuminate the art of taking calculated risks.

A Tightrope Walk of Financial Challenges

As a young mother determined to make her mark in the corporate world, I knew intimately the burden of financial challenges. The weight of providing for my family, combined with my relentless ambition, demanded a delicate balance. It was not just a pursuit of personal success; it was the responsibility of securing a brighter future for my children.

One calculated risk that became a defining moment was the decision to relocate my family from St. Louis to the bustling city of Chicago. This move was not merely about a change of scenery; it symbolized chasing financial opportunities and breaking free from the constraints of a limited income. Chicago promised not only a higher income but also demanded a significant leap of faith—a move that would either propel us toward success or present formidable challenges.

The decision to move to Chicago underlined the paramount importance of taking risks in the pursuit of financial independence. It was a bold step that showcased my determination to provide a more stable future for my family.

Strategic Career Moves: From Audit to Due Diligence

My journey at PricewaterhouseCoopers (PwC) was punctuated by a series of strategic career moves, each meticulously planned to maximize my earning potential and propel me closer to my dreams. I realized early on that financial freedom was a critical component of my aspirations, and I was willing to tread unconventional paths to achieve it.

One of the most pivotal career transitions was the shift from an audit role to due diligence. This strategic move promised a higher income but came at the cost of longer work hours and increased responsibilities. It was a calculated risk that rigorously tested my resolve, yet the potential rewards far outweighed the challenges. This leap of faith marked a significant milestone in my journey toward financial independence.

The Art of Calculated Risks

My journey in corporate America has taught me that calculated risks are not reckless gambles; they are strategic choices rooted in research, foresight, and unwavering determination. They serve as stepping stones to progress and catalysts for personal and professional growth. Here are the essential lessons I've gathered along the way:

- Lesson 1: Do Your Homework
    - Before embarking on any risk, comprehensive research is paramount. Understanding potential benefits and drawbacks is crucial. Consulting with

mentors, colleagues, and industry experts provides invaluable insights. A well-researched risk is more likely to yield positive results.

- Lesson 2: Define Your Goals
  - Clearly articulating your objectives is essential. Whether it's an increase in income, a more challenging role, or the pursuit of a coveted leadership position, well-defined goals serve as guiding stars, steering your decision-making process and instilling a sense of purpose.
- Lesson 3: Embrace Change
  - Calculated risks often require stepping out of your comfort zone. Embrace change as an opportunity for growth and personal development. Recognize that it's often in moments of discomfort that we discover our greatest strengths and capabilities.
- Lesson 4: Be Persistent
  - Not every risk will lead to immediate success. Maintaining persistence and resilience in the

face of setbacks is crucial. The path to success is rarely linear, but your unwavering determination will carry you through even the most challenging times.

- Lesson 5: Network and Seek Guidance
  - Networking with mentors and colleagues who possess experience in taking calculated risks can be transformative. Their guidance and support provide invaluable insights and help navigate the intricate corporate landscape.

A Black Woman's Perspective

As a Black woman striving for success in the corporate world, my perspective on calculated risks is deeply rooted in the unique challenges and opportunities I've encountered. I've confronted biases and stereotypes, but I've also harnessed the strength within me to persevere. My journey is a testament to the fact that diversity is an asset, and breaking barriers is a noble pursuit.

The Path Forward

This comprehensive chapter underscores the transformative power of taking calculated risks in the pursuit of success. It serves as a guiding light for those navigating the intricate terrain of corporate America and beyond. Calculated risks are not mere gambles; they are strategic choices that can redefine your career, lead to unparalleled growth, and empower you to seize control of your destiny.

In the profound words of Maya Angelou, "You may not control all the events that happen to you, but you can decide not to be reduced by them." Each calculated risk is a step forward in shaping the narrative of your success, and my journey is a testament to the infinite possibilities that await those who dare to take them.

Chapter 7: When to Make a Move in Your Career

In the intricate dance of corporate America, the decision of when to make a career move is a nuanced art. This chapter is dedicated to exploring the delicate balance between job stability and seizing opportunities, with added insights into the importance of seeking advice from others and carefully evaluating job offers.

The Value of Job Stability

Job stability is a cornerstone of a successful career, and my journey in public accounting exemplifies its importance. During my eight-year tenure at PwC, I honed my skills and deepened my expertise. I nurtured valuable relationships and solidified my reputation as a reliable and capable professional. This stability was essential for building a strong foundation in my career.

Staying at PwC for eight years was not merely a decision driven by comfort; it was a conscious choice to build a solid foundation in public accounting. It allowed me to grow, excel, and establish myself as a leader within the organization. The stability I gained during this time would later prove invaluable as I considered more significant career moves.

Embracing Opportunities for Growth

While job stability is vital, seizing the right opportunities at the right time can be equally transformative. My transition to Ernst & Young (EY) after eight years at PwC was a calculated move in public accounting. It presented the chance to step into a more advanced leadership role and increase my income substantially. This transition underscored the importance of recognizing when a change can propel your career to new heights.

EY provided a fresh perspective and a different corporate culture within the realm of public accounting. It challenged me to adapt, grow, and expand my horizons. The three years at EY were a period of intense learning and development, setting the stage for my next significant career move.

Making the Leap to Sterling Group

The decision to transition to Sterling Group, a middle-market private equity firm, as their Controller in public accounting was not made lightly. It was fueled by the promise of a substantially higher income and an opportunity to lead a dynamic finance team. This leap represented a calculated risk, a strategic career move that aligned with my aspirations.

Before making this pivotal move, I engaged in a thorough evaluation process. I sought advice from mentors, colleagues, and industry experts. Their perspectives were invaluable in weighing the pros and cons of the job offer. This highlighted the importance of tapping into the wisdom of others when making critical career decisions.

One remarkable aspect of changing jobs that often goes unnoticed is the opportunity to negotiate. When considering a new role, you're in a prime position to discuss compensation and benefits that align with your worth and aspirations. This is a golden opportunity to double-dip on raises and secure a more favorable financial future.

Lessons in Timing

The decision of when to make a career move in public accounting is nuanced and depends on various factors, including your personal goals and circumstances. Here are some key lessons I've learned:

- Lesson 1: Assess Your Goals
  - Before considering a career move, take time to assess your professional and financial goals within the realm of public accounting. Define what success means to you and what steps will lead you there.
- Lesson 2: Evaluate Opportunities
  - When presented with an opportunity, evaluate it rigorously. Consider the potential for increased income, advanced leadership roles, and personal growth. Ensure the move aligns with your long-term aspirations within public accounting.
- Lesson 3: Prioritize Financial Stability
  - Financial stability is a critical consideration in public accounting. A career move should enhance your income potential, not jeopardize it. Calculate the financial impact and weigh it against the potential benefits.
- Lesson 4: Seek Advice
  - Don't underestimate the power of seeking advice from mentors,

colleagues, and industry experts when making career decisions. Their insights can provide invaluable perspectives and guide you in the right direction.

- Lesson 5: Negotiate Wisely
  - When changing jobs, use the opportunity to negotiate for compensation and benefits that align with your worth and aspirations. Don't leave potential raises on the table; seize the chance to secure your financial future.

The Path Forward

In the words of Steve Jobs, "Your work is going to fill a large part of your life, and the only way to be truly satisfied is to do what you believe is great work. And the only way to do great work is to love what you do." Each transition in my career within public accounting was a deliberate step toward doing what I believed was great work and achieving personal and financial satisfaction.

This chapter serves as a guide for navigating the intricate balance between job stability and seizing opportunities within public accounting.

It underscores the importance of making strategic career moves that align with your aspirations and lead to personal and financial fulfillment. In the ever-evolving world of public accounting and corporate America, finding the right timing for your career moves can be a transformative journey toward success.

Chapter 8: The Art of the Interviewing

As a Black woman striving to excel financially in the corporate world, interviews have been pivotal moments in my career journey. They have been the gateways to new opportunities, enabling me to navigate the intricate landscape of corporate America. In this chapter, I will share the secrets I've learned about excelling in interviews, drawing from my experiences when leaving PricewaterhouseCoopers (PwC) and Ernst & Young (EY). These insights are not only applicable to Black women but to anyone seeking to make their mark in the professional world.

Crafting a Tailored Resume: Your Unique Narrative

Your resume is the first impression you make on potential employers, and for someone like me, it was the key to unlocking doors to financial success. Here's how I crafted a resume that not only showcased my skills but also conveyed my unique narrative:

1. Highlighting Achievements: Instead of merely listing job responsibilities, I put

my achievements front and center. Numbers and statistics became my allies in demonstrating the impact I could make.

2. Tailoring for the Role: Each job application was an opportunity to tailor my resume. I focused on experiences and skills that were directly relevant to the position I was pursuing, showcasing my adaptability and resourcefulness.

3. Telling My Story: My resume wasn't just a document; it was a story of my career journey. I explained how each role had led to the next, painting a picture of my growth and evolution.

4. Using Action Verbs: To project confidence, I began bullet points with powerful action verbs like "achieved," "managed," or "implemented." This made my resume more engaging and dynamic.

5. Quantifying Achievements: Whenever possible, I quantified my achievements. For example, I proudly stated that I "Increased sales revenue by 30% in six months." This not only showcased my accomplishments but also painted a vivid picture of my capabilities.

Mastering the Art of Body Language: Confidence in Every Glance

Interviews are not just about what you say but also how you present yourself. As a Black woman aiming to secure positions at PwC and EY, mastering the art of body language was crucial:

1. Maintaining Eye Contact: Establishing and maintaining eye contact was vital. It conveyed my confidence and showed that I was fully engaged in the conversation.
2. Wearing a Warm Expression: A warm and genuine smile became my secret weapon. It put both me and my interviewers at ease, creating a positive and welcoming atmosphere.
3. Strong Posture: I made sure to sit or stand with a straight posture. This not only projected confidence but also demonstrated respect for the interviewers and the process.
4. Active Listening: Non-verbal cues also include active listening. Nodding and offering small affirmations showed that I was fully engaged in the conversation.
5. Appropriate Hand Gestures: I used hand gestures sparingly and

appropriately to emphasize points. Overdoing it can be distracting, so I found a balance that worked for me.

Asking the Right Questions: Demonstrating Interest and Preparedness

Asking thoughtful questions during an interview not only showcases your interest but also provides valuable insights into the role and company culture. Here are some strategies I used:

1. Researching the Company: Before each interview, I delved deep into the company's history, values, and recent news. This allowed me to tailor my questions and demonstrate my genuine interest.
2. Questioning the Role: I asked about the specific responsibilities of the role, showing that I was already envisioning myself in the position and considering how I could contribute.
3. Inquiring About Company Culture: Questions about company culture and team dynamics revealed my commitment to a harmonious work environment and my ability to adapt to different settings.

4. Seeking Feedback: Towards the end of the interview, I often asked about the company's expectations and the potential for growth within the role. This indicated my long-term commitment and ambition.

The Path Forward: Mastering the Art of the Interview

Interviews are not just checkpoints in your career journey; they are opportunities to shape your destiny. Whether you're a Black woman like me or anyone striving for financial excellence, mastering the art of the interview is crucial. Your resume, body language, and questions should all reflect your unique narrative and your unwavering commitment to success.

In the wise words of Oprah Winfrey, "The biggest adventure you can take is to live the life of your dreams." Interviews are the vehicles that can take you on that adventure. Use them wisely, and watch as your dreams become your reality.

Chapter 9: The Power of Leverage

As a Black woman navigating the corporate landscape, my journey has been a testament to the power of leverage. In this chapter, I will share how I negotiated my way through career transitions, leveraging job offers from top companies to not only earn the respect I deserved but also secure the compensation necessary to support my family. These experiences, which included multiple interviews when leaving PricewaterhouseCoopers (PwC) and Ernst & Young (EY), reflect the determination and strategic thinking required to excel financially while breaking barriers.

Navigating Career Transitions: The Catalyst for Leverage

The decision to leave a stable and well-established workplace like PwC or EY is never easy, especially for someone striving to excel financially and support their family. However, it's during these transitions that the power of leverage becomes undeniably valuable.

The Catalyst for Leverage

Leaving my comfort zone at PwC and EY was motivated by the desire to seek better opportunities, both in terms of income and career growth. However, these decisions were not made lightly. I knew that to secure the best offers at the best salaries, I needed to leverage my unique skill set and experiences.

The Art of Multiple Interviews

When contemplating these career transitions, I didn't settle for the first job offer that came my way. Instead, I embarked on a journey of multiple interviews, not just to evaluate potential employers but also to create a powerful negotiating position.

Each interview provided insights into the company's culture, expectations, and growth potential. It allowed me to assess whether the company aligned with my values and career aspirations, critical factors for someone committed to financial success.

Having multiple job offers gave me the leverage to negotiate better terms, from salary to benefits and even work-life balance. I had the confidence to advocate for myself and ensure that I received what I deserved.

The Power of Leverage in Negotiation

Negotiation isn't just about asking for more; it's about demonstrating your value and your commitment to your financial goals. When armed with multiple job offers, I learned several key strategies:

Understanding the market value for your skills and experience is crucial. Research industry salary benchmarks and be prepared to articulate why you deserve a certain compensation package.

Leverage your unique skills, experiences, and achievements to stand out. Show how you can bring immediate value to the company, making it clear that you're not just another candidate but a game-changer.

Be Confident but Flexible

Confidence is essential, but flexibility can be equally powerful. Sometimes, it's not just about salary but also about benefits, work arrangements, or professional development opportunities. Be open to negotiation on multiple fronts.

Negotiation can take time, and it's crucial to be patient. Sometimes, employers need a little extra time to meet your demands, so don't rush the process.

The Path Forward: Leveraging Your Financial Success

In the words of Maya Angelou, "You may not control all the events that happen to you, but you can decide not to be reduced by them." My journey as a Black woman in corporate America has been defined by this resilience and determination. Navigating career transitions, mastering the art of multiple interviews, and leveraging job offers were all instrumental in my pursuit of financial excellence.

This chapter serves as a testament to the power of leverage, a tool that can propel you toward your financial goals while ensuring you receive the respect and compensation you deserve. Whether you're a Black woman like me or anyone striving for financial success, remember that you hold the keys to your destiny. Leverage them wisely, and watch as you unlock doors to a brighter financial future.

Chapter 10: Starting Over

In the complex tapestry of a career, there are threads of success and challenges, moments of triumph and setbacks. This chapter, titled "Starting Over," is a pivotal juncture in my journey. It was a time when I faced the unexpected — getting laid off from my interim CFO role at Sterling Group. However, little did I know that this setback would open the door to a new venture and a chance to leverage all the experience I had gained from my years at PricewaterhouseCoopers (PwC) and Ernst & Young (EY).

The Layoff: An Unforeseen Twist

Getting laid off is never easy, especially when you've worked tirelessly to climb the corporate ladder. My role as interim CFO at Sterling Group was, in many ways, the culmination of years of hard work and dedication. However, life has a way of throwing unexpected curveballs, and the layoff was one such twist in my professional journey.

The Impact on My Family and Personal Life

The layoff from Sterling Group had a profound impact on my family, friends, and personal life.

It was a period of uncertainty and adjustment. While it came with its share of challenges, it also offered an unforeseen opportunity for me to recalibrate my life's balance.

As my husband and I faced this unexpected turn of events, we knew we had to have a candid conversation about our future. This was a pivotal moment that required careful consideration. Should I seek another job or take a leap of faith and start my own consulting firm? This decision had significant implications not just for me but for our entire family.

As we delved into our discussion, one idea loomed large in our minds: generational wealth-building. We realized that entrepreneurship and starting my own consulting firm could potentially be a pathway to creating a better legacy for our children and grandchildren. It was a chance to leave a lasting impact and provide financial security for generations to come.

Amidst the uncertainty that followed my layoff, I made a bold decision — to start my own consulting firm. Drawing upon the wealth of experience I had gained during my years at PwC and EY, I knew I had the skills and knowledge to make it a success.

Leveraging My Expertise

The years spent in consulting had equipped me with a deep understanding of financial strategies, business operations, and the intricacies of corporate America. I saw this as a chance to leverage that expertise and offer valuable insights to clients.

Starting my consulting firm wasn't just a career move; it was a financial decision that would change the trajectory of my life. The income potential was substantial, and it allowed me to provide for my family while also pursuing my dreams.

Striving for Excellence, On My Terms

Launching my own consulting firm was not without its challenges. It required dedication, perseverance, and a commitment to excellence on my terms. As I ventured into this new chapter, I realized that I could finally spend more time with my family after years of being away due to my demanding career.

One of the most significant benefits of starting my consulting firm was achieving a healthier work-life balance. It allowed me to be there for my family and friends in ways that my previous roles had not permitted.

Surprisingly, as I focused on my consulting firm, my income surpassed even the levels I had achieved in my corporate roles. It was a testament to the potential for financial success when you're in control of your destiny.

The Path Forward: Embracing New Beginnings

In the words of Oprah Winfrey, "Think like a queen. A queen is not afraid to fail. Failure is another stepping stone to greatness." The layoff from Sterling Group was a temporary setback, but it paved the way for a new beginning filled with possibilities.

This chapter serves as a reminder that life's twists and turns can lead us to unexpected places. Starting my own consulting firm was a bold leap into the unknown, but it was a decision that allowed me to regain control of my life, achieve financial success, and cherish the moments with my loved ones.

As I embraced this new beginning, I carried with me the lessons learned from every chapter of my journey. Each experience had shaped me into the resilient, determined Black woman I am today, always striving for excellence and making the most of every opportunity life presents. It was a reminder that setbacks are merely stepping stones to something better, and with the right vision, determination, and support from loved ones, we can build a legacy that extends beyond our lifetime.

Chapter 11: Achieving the Dream

Throughout my journey, I've encountered hurdles, overcome challenges, and embraced opportunities. But perhaps the most fulfilling moment came when I realized a dream that had been etched into my heart since childhood — the dream of buying a home in my dream neighborhood. It was a culmination of years of hard work, determination, and unwavering commitment to achieving my goals. This chapter is a reflection on my remarkable achievements and the profound joy of realizing a lifelong dream.

The Childhood Dream

From a young age, I carried a vision with me — a vision of living in a neighborhood that symbolized success, comfort, and opportunity. My mother, a dedicated teacher and single parent, had instilled in me the importance of education and aspiration. She and I would often drive past this neighborhood, admiring the beautiful homes with sprawling lawns and the promise of an excellent education within its borders.

At that time, the idea of living in such a neighborhood was as improbable as winning the lottery, maybe even less so. But my mother, ever the realist, told me that she hoped I could achieve it one day. It was a dream that we shared, an aspiration born from hope and the belief that with hard work and dedication, anything was possible.

The journey to achieving this dream was long and arduous, marked by obstacles, challenges, and moments of doubt. It was a path that required tenacity, resilience, and an unyielding commitment to success. From an early age, I faced adversity, becoming a mother at a young age and dropping out of college. However, I knew deep down that these circumstances did not define my destiny.

Returning to College

At the age of 28, I made a life-changing decision—to return to college. It was a daunting prospect, especially with a husband and three children to support. But I believed that education was the key to a brighter future for my family. I graduated just before turning 30, ranking number one in the business school.

My journey led me to PwC, where I navigated the complexities of corporate America. Despite struggles in my first year, I achieved early promotions through hard work and dedication.

The Best Version of Myself

To me, being the best meant more than just meeting expectations; it meant surpassing them. This ethos was instilled in me by my father, who emphasized the importance of knowledge and the power it brings.

I went beyond technical skills, delving into self-improvement, studying books like "How to Win Friends and Influence People," and developing emotional intelligence and cultural dexterity.

Stepping into the corporate world at PwC, I learned the value of excellence. It was a demanding environment, especially for a Black woman, and I knew I had to work doubly hard to excel.

Despite moments of adversity, I clung to my father's wisdom, striving to be the best and to possess the knowledge that would empower me. From excelling in interviews to forming meaningful relationships, I left no stone unturned.

Owning My Career

Owning my career meant stepping out of my comfort zone, networking with peers, and positioning myself as a leader. Understanding corporate culture and navigating it deftly became crucial.

After eight years at PwC and three at EY, I knew it was time for a change. I received job offers from prestigious companies, but I was discerning. I sought power moves that justified leaving my current role. Job stability was a key factor. I didn't want to jump from one position to another without a plan. I aimed for strategic moves that would advance my career and financial goals.

A Dream Realized

And then, almost miraculously, it happened. After working at Sterling Group for two years, I received my first six figure bonus. My credit had finally recovered and I was finally able to realize my dream. On August 9, 2016, almost 14 years after receiving my accounting degree, I bought a home in my dream neighborhood. It was an achievement beyond my wildest expectations.

This wasn't a goal I set when I decided to return to school, but achieving it was just as sweet. It was a testament to the belief that with determination and a relentless pursuit of excellence, dreams can be within reach.

I recalled those same powerful words of Harriet Beecher Stowe, "Never give up, for that is just the place and time that the tide will turn." My journey was proof that your past doesn't define your future. With dedication and a relentless pursuit of excellence, even your most cherished dreams can come true.

Epilogue - Your Destiny Awaits

As I reflect upon my journey, I'm reminded of the incredible power that determination, resilience, and the pursuit of excellence can have in shaping one's destiny. This epilogue is a culmination of my inspirational story, a reminder that regardless of the obstacles you face, your destiny awaits, ready to be shaped by your unwavering commitment to success.

Life is a journey filled with twists and turns, unexpected challenges, and moments of triumph. My own path was far from linear, marked by setbacks, doubts, and hurdles. I faced adversity early in life, became a parent at a young age, and dropped out of college. It seemed as though the odds were stacked against me.

But within those challenges lay the seeds of my determination. At 28, I made the life-altering decision to return to college, and I graduated as the top student in the business school just before turning 30. This moment marked the beginning of a journey that would lead me through the corridors of corporate America.

My tenure at PricewaterhouseCoopers (PwC) was marked by challenges and triumphs. In my early years, I faced the risk of being "counseled out." However, I clung to the belief that I could be a top performer, and I achieved early promotions. With each passing year, I gained clarity about what I wanted to achieve in my career and life. I honed my interviewing skills, formed meaningful relationships, and navigated corporate culture with finesse. My career took me from PwC to EY and ultimately to Sterling Group, each transition bringing new challenges and opportunities.

Unexpectedly, my journey took an unexpected turn when I was laid off from my interim CFO role at Sterling Group. It was a setback, but I saw it as an opportunity to start my own consulting firm. Consultations with my husband highlighted the potential for generational wealth-building.

Starting my consulting firm wasn't just about financial success; it was about building a legacy for our children and grandchildren. It was a chance to leave an indelible mark and provide for generations to come.

The crowning achievement of my journey came when I fulfilled my childhood dream of buying a home in my dream neighborhood. It was a testament to the unwavering determination that had guided me throughout my life. My story serves as a reminder that your past does not determine your future. With dedication, resilience, and a relentless pursuit of excellence, you can overcome adversity and achieve your dreams in corporate America.

In the words of Maya Angelou, "You may encounter many defeats, but you must not be defeated." Your destiny awaits, and it's yours to shape. As you embark on your own journey in the corporate world, remember the lessons from my story — the importance of knowledge, the power of leverage, and the pursuit of excellence.

Your path may be unpredictable, but with determination, resilience, and the unwavering belief in yourself, you can overcome any obstacle. Your destiny is within reach, ready to be shaped by your relentless commitment to success.

Throughout my journey, I offered practical advice, rules of engagement for corporate success, and the motivation to persevere despite obstacles. My story encapsulates the intersection of dreams, destiny, and debits and credits, offering valuable lessons for those seeking to change their lives and find their own path to success. As my story concludes, I pass the torch to you, my beautiful sister, to embrace your own journey, face your challenges head-on, and fulfill your dreams.